The Inferno

Dante Alighieri

Henderson County Public Library

Copyright © BiblioBazaar, LLC

BiblioBazaar Reproduction Series: Our goal at BiblioBazaar is to help readers, educators and researchers by bringing back in print hard-to-find original publications at a reasonable price and, at the same time, preserve the legacy of literary history. The following book represents an authentic reproduction of the text as printed by the original publisher and may contain prior copyright references. While we have attempted to accurately maintain the integrity of the original work(s), from time to time there are problems with the original book scan that may result in minor errors in the reproduction, including imperfections such as missing and blurred pages, poor pictures, markings and other reproduction issues beyond our control. Because this work is culturally important, we have made it available as a part of our commitment to protecting, preserving and promoting the world's literature.

All of our books are in the "public domain" and many are derived from Open Source projects dedicated to digitizing historic literature. We believe that when we undertake the difficult task of re-creating them as attractive, readable and affordable books, we further the mutual goal of sharing these works with a larger audience. A portion of Bibliobazaar profits go back to Open Source projects in the form of a donation to the groups that do this important work around the world. If you would like to make a donation to these worthy Open Source projects, or would just like to get more information about these important initiatives, please visit www.bibliobazaar.com/opensource.

THE INFERNO

OF

DANTE ALIGHIERI.

TRANSLATED INTO ENGLISH VERSE, WITH NOTES,

BY

ERNEST RIDSDALE ELLABY, M.A.,

FELLOW OF WADHAM COLLEGE, OXFORD, AND OF LINCOLN'S
INN, BARRISTER-AT-LAW.

CANTOS I–X.

LONDON :
BICKERS AND SON, 1, LEICESTER SQUARE, W.C.
1874.

TO

THE RIGHT HONOURABLE

HENRY, EARL GREY, K.G.,

&c., &c.

THIS VOLUME

IS INSCRIBED WITH RESPECT

BY

THE TRANSLATOR.

Corrigenda.

Page 23, v. 103.—

>*For* "The Holy One of Heaven—the earth
>   And human kind—"

>*Read*—"The dread Lord of heaven and earth—
>   The human race—"

Page 54, v. 2.—*For* "turret's" *read*—"tower's."

Page 58, v. 98.—

>*For* "Restored my safety, and hast led
>   My steps thro'"

>*Read*—"Restored my failing strength and brought
>   Me forth from"

Page 59, v. 112.—

>*For* "I could not hear the words, &c.

>*Read*—"I could not hear his parley; but he stood
>   Not long with them in conference before
>   They all ran back pell-mell within the walls."

Page 68, v. 6.—*For* "longing wish" *read*—"deep desires."

PREFACE.

———o———

THE first three Cantos of the following Translation are—with the exception of a very few lines, in which weak rhymes have been discarded—executed in the 'terza rima.' In translating the lists of names in the fourth Canto, I found that it would be impossible to preserve this metre without deviating from the original to an extent which it seemed to me would involve a greater evil than the sacrifice of the rhyme. I was thus led to inquire whether the maintenance of an unbroken series of final rhymes was really as indispensable as I had previously supposed. The fact that the most richly harmonious specimens of English poetry are to be found—as I think will generally be admitted—not in any of our rhyming poets, but in the blank verse of Milton, would seem to indicate that rhyme is of secondary importance in poetical composition. The musical effect of verse, whether rhymed or unrhymed, is, in fact, produced by the harmonious disposition of *all* its con-

stituent sounds. These considerations suggested to me the
method of versification employed in the later Cantos, in
which I have endeavoured, by varying the harmony in
imitation of the more ornate passages in the Paradise Lost
and Paradise Regained, by retaining the movement in
triplets, and connecting the triplets by means either of a
final rhyme or half-rhyme or of some internal harmony, to
combine something of the freedom of Miltonic verse with
the two most essential characteristics of the Italian metre,
viz., the separation of the triplets, and their connection
by a common sound.[1]

In translating I have striven to be as literal as possible
Nor have I in any case allowed myself to deviate to
any considerable extent from the words of Dante, unless
it has appeared to me that such deviation is better
calculated than a more literal rendering to express
either the full meaning or the harmony of the original,
or the actual thought of the Poet, as opposed to the

---

[1] A careful analysis of Milton's versification, suggested, after the
completion of the third Canto, by my having accidentally observed
(while studying his poetry in connection with the Miltonic epitaph
discovered by Professor Morley, and published in the *Times* in
1868) a considerable number of final rhymes in his blank verse (see,
e.g. P. L. i. 183-191, iv. 306-311, vii. 548-573), confirmed me in the
opinion that the method of harmonising, which I have adopted in the
later Cantos, is no illegitimate extension of the Miltonic method.

particular expression which the rhyme has led him to adopt.

In the preparation of the Notes I have been chiefly indebted to the Commentary of Signor Brunone Bianchi, which was recommended to me by Count Aurelio Saffi. I have also derived assistance from the Translations and Commentaries of Longfellow, Cary, Wright, and Pollock; the French Translation of M. Louis Ratisbonne; and the superb edition of the Inferno by the late Lord Vernon.

Other Cantos I have translated, and hope to publish. Those comprised in the present volume have already undergone several revisions since they were first printed. I respectfully submit them to the judgment of the reader.

November, 1874.

THE INFERNO.

CANTO I.

Nel mezzo del cammin.

—

ARGUMENT.

DANTE is lost in a wood. Arriving at the base of a hill, whose
summit is illumined by the rays of the rising sun, he beholds three
wild beasts on the heights above him. Returning in alarm, he is
met by Virgil, whose aid he implores. Virgil informs him that
he must traverse the unseen world, if he would escape the perils
of the wood. He offers himself to guide the Poet through Hell
and Purgatory. Beatrice would be his guide into Paradise.

ON life's mid-way—ere half my days were o'er—

    All in a darksome wood[1] I roved astray,

    Wherein the way of truth was seen no more.

Ah me! 'twere a sad task and hard to say

    How wild that woodland was, how sharp, how strong   5

    Its growth, which ev'n in thought renews dismay.

---

[1] Error.

Does there to death such bitterness belong ?

    Yet wondrous things athwart my path that lay,

    And good which there I found shall wake my song.

How first I enter'd there I scarce can say ;   10

    So heedless was I and so full of sleep

    That hour wherein I swerved from the straight way.

But soon as I had gain'd a hill-side steep—[2]

    There where that dark and dreary valley ended,

    That made my heart to grieve and eyes to weep—   15

Lo ! as I gazed, over its slope descended

    Vesture of light from the heaven-wanderer,

    Upon whose course are all things else suspended.

Then tranquillized a little was the fear

    That in the deep lake of my heart [3] had lain   20

    All that long night of anguish and despair.

And like as one forth from the sea's domain

    Escaped unto the shore with labouring breath

    Turns back and gazes at the perilous main ;

---

[2] Truth. Politically, the ideal form of government for Italy and mankind—in Dante's opinion, an universal monarchy, seated at Rome, with the Pope as spiritual head.

[3] Variously interpreted :—by Signor Bianchi, as referring to the stagnation of the blood in the vessels of the heart caused by terror ; by M. Louis Ratisbonne, as 'le lac agité de mon cœur ; ' and by Long-fellow as 'the deep mountain tarn of his heart, dark with its own depth, and the shadows hanging over it.'

So did my spirit, that still sank beneath 25

  Its anguish, backward turn to view the place

  Wherein none else entering had 'scaped from death.

I stay'd a while to rest my weariness;

  Then, moving gradual o'er a gentle rise,[4]

  My way I took thro' that wide wilderness. 30

And lo! just where the emerald steep 'gan rise,

  A Leopard[5] light of foot, quick-moving, gay

  With speckled skin, unto my wondering eyes

Appear'd, nor vanish'd, rather did my way

  Perplex and hinder so that many a time 35

  I turnèd to go back in deep dismay.

It was the hour of the morning's prime;

  And the sun clomb up those self-same stars[6] among

  Wherewith encompassèd he rose sublime

---

[4] The soul enters upon the quest after truth with confidence, meeting with no difficulty at the outset, and having no consciousness of the obstacles which lie in the way.

[5] Envy. Inf. vi. 50, 74; xv. 68. Otherwise, with Longfellow, and others, Worldly Pleasure.

The imagery in verses 31-54 is evidently borrowed from Jeremiah v. 6. ' Wherefore a lion out of the forest shall slay them, a wolf of the evenings shall spoil them, a leopard shall watch over their cities: every one that goeth out thence shall be torn in pieces.'

[6] The stars of Aries. 'The world was anciently believed to have been created in the spring. "Ver illud erat." Georg. II. 336.' Wright.

When Love Divine those glorious worlds along   40
   Their orbits first impell'd.   The sweet spring-tide,
   The birds that round me tuned their matin song,
Were cause of hope that from that speckled hide
   No harm would spring :[7] yet not so that my dread
   Return'd not when a Lion[8] I espied,   45
That onward came right in my path with head
   Aloft and glaring wild with hungry eye,
   That ev'n the air seem'd to shrink back afraid.
And a She-wolf,[9] whose leanness seem'd to be
   Full fraught with all inordinate desire,   50
   And many a soul had fill'd with misery,
Wrought in my spirit such confusion dire—
   So fearfully her grisly form did show—
   That I all hope resign'd of mounting higher.
And like as one that kindleth with the glow   55
   Of gain—and then, to mar his full delight,
   There cometh loss—he sinks o'erwhelm'd with woe ;
So by that beast was I dishearten'd quite,
   That still with stealthy tread approaching nigh
   Downward involved me in the shades of night.   60

---

[7] The hour of the day, and the season of the year, induced the hope that the Leopard would prove harmless. This animal is said to retire to its den at sun-rise in the spring. Allegorically, envy is subdued by the tranquillizing influence of the morning, and by love inspired by the season.

Thus hurrying down the shelter'd ground to reach
    Before my wearied eyes appearèd one
    Who thro' long silence seem'd bereft of speech.[10]
When I descried him in the desert lone,
    'Have pity on me!' I cried out, 'whate'er   65
    Thou art, or living man, or shade undone.'
He made response ; 'Not living man, tho' once
    Terrestrial air I drew—Italian-born
    Of Lombard ancestors in Mantua fair,
When mightiest Julius did the world adorn :   70
    I lived at Rome 'neath good Augustus' sway,
    When mankind groan'd in bondage all forlorn
Of lying gods.   'Twas I who sang the lay
    Of just Anchises' son, who came from Troy,
    When Ilium's proud towers in ashes lay.   75
Why lingerest thou where grovelling cares annoy?
    What hinders thee to scale the beauteous mountain,
    Which is the source and giver of all joy?'
'Art thou then Virgil, that perennial fountain,
    Whence welleth out of speech so large a river?'   80
    I answer'd all abash'd.   'O light and glory

---

[8] Pride.   [9] Avarice.

[10] This line is said to refer to the neglect of classical literature in Italy during the dark ages.

Of other bards! now may the long endeavour
  And the deep love with which I ponder'd thro'
  Thy sacred page avail me! Thou wert ever
My Master and my chief Inspirer!—thou   85
  Alone, for 'twas from thee I won the fair
  Style that with honour's wreath adorns my brow.
Yon wolf, that made me turn, still hovering there
  Thou seest : save me from her, renownèd sage,
  Whose presence shakes each pulse, each vein with fear.' 90
' Meet is it thou another pilgrimage
  Should'st make,' he answer'd, when he saw my tears,
  ' Would'st thou escape this desert, and the rage
Of yonder beast.[11]   For whosoe'er appears
  Upon the slope of this delightful hill,   95
  Hindering his upward course she rends and tears
And slays outright :—nor gluts her ravenous will,
  But after each repast—so dire, so dread
  Her devilish nature—grows more hungry still.
With many a bestial creature she doth wed,   100
  And shall with more till that Greyhound arise,[12]
  Who will afflict her sore, and bruise her head.

---

[11] Contemplation, and not action, was the vocation of the Poet.
It was indirectly—by means of his poem—that he was to benefit his
country and mankind.

[12] Comparing this passage with Parad. xvii. 76—90, and especially

Not of the earth or earthly vanities,

    But wisdom, virtue, love his food shall be :

    'Twixt either Feltro[13] his dominion lies.   105

Deliverer of down-fallen Italy,[14]

    For whom died brave Camilla, virgin pure,

    Turnus, Euryalus, and Nisus—he

Thro' every land and town with scourge severe

    Back to the mouth of Hell yon wolf shall chase,   110

    Whence Envy-born she sprang.—Now, pondering, clear

My mind discerns that thou thro' Heaven's grace

    Wilt follow me thy Guide ordain'd to bear

    Thee hence into an everlasting place,

Where thou wilt hear the shriekings of despair,   115

    And see the ancient spirits rack'd with pain—

    Each one a second death invoking there.

---

the line
        ' Questi non ciberà terra nè peltro'
with the lines
        ' Parran faville della sua virtute
          In non curar d' argento, nè d' affanni,'
it seems probable that the Veltro, or Greyhound, is intended to denote
Can Grande della Scala, who is unquestionably the person referred to
in the above passage from the Paradiso. Can Grande was one of
Dante's chief friends in exile. He was called ' catulus Veronæ.'
Other references to him are traced in Purg. xx.13 ; xxxiii. 40.

    [13] Feltro, in the Marca Trivigiana, and Montefeltro, in Romagna.

    [14] ' Umile Italia.' So interpreted by Buti. Cary and others think

And thou shalt see those others, who are fain

  In fire to purge them, hopeful in the end

  Among the Blessed entrance to obtain.   120

Unto whose glory if thou would'st ascend,

  Another soul[15] must come worthier than I :

  Thither with her may'st thou thy footsteps wend.

For that dread Emperor, who reigns on high,

  Suffers me not—for that I did rebel   125

  Against His law[16]—within the empyreal sky

To lead thee.   There in lofty citadel

  Enthronèd He the universe doth sway.

  Oh, blest are they with Him elect to dwell !'

Outspake I then, and said ; ' Poet, I pray   130

  Thee by that Holy One thou did'st not know,

  That I from this and greater evil may

---

that the expression was suggested by Virgil's

    ' Cum procul obscuros colles, humilemque videmus

      Italiam.'

                  Æn. III. 522.

[15] Beatrice, the daughter of Folco Portinari, whom Dante met for the first time in A.D. 1274, when he was nine years old. He describes this meeting and its effect upon him at the opening of ' La vita nuova.'

[16] Dante's words, ' ribellante alla sua legge,' must be taken to mean simply—as Signor Bianchi remarks—' *alieno* dalla sua legge o *non seguace* di essa.' Otherwise the passage is directly at variance with the statement in Canto iv., that the spirits in Limbo, of whom Virgil was one, had not ' sinned.' See Cant. iv. 34, &c.

Escape, lead thou me where thou said'st, that so
   These eyes may see where Peter sits enshrined
   In glory, and those spirits whelm'd in woe.'   135
Then movèd he, and I held on behind.

CANTO II.

Lo giorno se n' andava.

—

ARGUMENT.

DANTE fears that his strength will prove insufficient for the enterprise. 'It was reasonable,' he argues, 'that Æneas and St. Paul, who were respectively concerned in laying and strengthening the foundations of the Roman Empire and the Christian Church, should traverse the unseen world; but what was his claim to so high a privilege?' Virgil revives the confidence of the Poet by relating how he had been visited by Beatrice, and sent by her to rescue him from the wood; and how St. Mary the Virgin and St. Lucy had also intervened on his behalf.

Now day declined, and Night with dusky wing
   Descending lull'd to rest the labour-wearied
   Creatures of earth, when I alone prepared
Myself to endure heart-piercing agony—
   The terrors of the wild tempestuous way—   5
   Deep graven on the unerring memory.

Ye sacred nine! aid my adventurous lay.

   Tell, O my mind, that which did there betide me,

   And all thy native nobleness display.

I thus broke silence ; 'Poet, that dost guide me,   10

   Weigh well my merit, if it sufficient be,

   Ere thou unto this perilous pass confide me.

Thou tell'st how Silvius' great sire,[1] while he

   Was yet corruptible, unto the place

   Immortal went, and was there sensibly.   15

Now, that the Enemy of all ill such grace

   On him bestow'd, measuring the high effect

   That was to ensue therefrom—the power—the race—

Appears not strange to one who can reflect,

   For that he was of Rome's imperial sway   20

   The original author in high heaven elect.

Which sway—not for itself alone—to say

   The truth—was stablish'd for the holy place,

   Where sitteth who succeeds to Peter's throne.

By this descent, made famous in thy story,   25

   He learn'd the sure foundation how to lay

   Of his success, and of the Papal glory.[2]

---

[1] Æneas.

[2] Æneid vi. 889-894.

Election's vessel [3] did this path essay,

 To gather confirmation for that Faith,

 Which guideth us into salvation's way.   30

That I the attempt should make—who sanctioneth ?

 I am not Paul, nor Rome's ancestral sage.

 Equal who deemeth me the paths of death

To traverse ? On that uncouth pilgrimage

 For me to go were a fond task and vain :   35

 Wise are thou, knowing all my fears presage.'

And like as one who what he will'd again

 Unwills, with new thoughts from his purpose bending,

 Which failing fadeth wholly from his brain ;

Ev'n so upon that darksome steep ascending   40

 My thoughts consumed the enterprise of good, .

 Embraced so soon, whereon my steps were wending.

' If rightly from thy language I conclude,'

 The shade of that great-minded one replied,

 ' Thy spirit is with cowardice imbued ;   45

Which oft-times leadeth men to turn aside

 In gloom of soul from loftiest enterprise,

 Like restive beasts with shadows terrified.

That thou may'st purge this film from off thine eyes,

 Thou shalt what brought me hither understand, 50

 And how I learn'd with thee to sympathise.

Erewhile in Limbo⁴ 'mid the hero band

   The irradiant form of one so fair was given

   To my rapt sight that I her swift command

Entreated.   Brighter than the star of even   55

   Her eyes were gleaming when she thus began

   With angel voice in the sweet speech of heaven ;

" O gentle spirit of the Mantuan,

   Whose name on earth with deathless glory blended

   Shall live for aye thro' time's remotest span,   60

My friend, alas ! by Fortune unbefriended,

   Is so perplex'd on the wild desert way

   That he thro' fear his onward course hath ended :

And now perchance hath gone so far astray

   That I to rescue him have risen in vain   65

   From what I hear the ethereal people say.

Thou therefore rise, and with the golden strain

   Of thy fair speech give timely aid, that so

   He may escape and I have rest again.

'Tis I—'tis Beatrice who bids thee go.   70

   I come from where I fain would be restored,

   By love impell'd which makes these tears to flow.

---

³ St. Paul. Acts ix. 15 ; and 2 Cor. xii. 2.

⁴ The first circle of Hell, described in Canto iv.

When I am in the presence of my Lord,

   I will rehearse thy praise before the throne."

   Ceasèd she then, and I took up the word ;   75

'O sovran Lady, by whose aid alone

   The feeble race of mánkind doth excel

   All else contain'd within heaven's lesser zone,[5]

This thy commandment pleaseth me so well,

   That were it done forthwith 'twere all too late :   80

   No need thy purpose more to unfold—but tell

The reason why thou dost not hesitate

   To venture down into this central gloom,

   Who longest to regain thy blessed seat ? "

" Seeing thou would'st into these depths presume,   85

   I will in brief unfold," she answer made,

   " Why without fear amid these shades I come.

'Tis meet to hold only those things in dread

   That tend to work another's woe or shame :

   All else thou may'st encounter undismay'd.   90

I am so framed by God—unto whose name

   Be all the praise—that this thy misery

   Touches me not, this restless quenchless flame.[6]

---

[5] The Lunar sphere of the Ptolemaic system.

[6] The 'hopeless desire' of the spirits in Limbo. Canto iv. 42

A saint[7] there is above, so piteously

   Bewails this hindrance[8] in her gentle breast,   95

   Ev'n Heaven is moved, and changed the stern decree.

She to Lucia[9] call'd, and made request,

   And said ; 'Now is thy faithful one in need

   Of thee : arise, and to his succour haste.'

Lucia, foe to every cruel deed,[10]   100

   Bestirr'd herself, and came unto the place

   Where I with the ancient Rachel sat, and said ;

'O Beatrice,[11] in whom Heaven's special grace

   Abounds, why aid'st thou not who lovèd thee

   So well, renouncing the vile herd and base?   105

Hearest thou not his piteous agony?

   Seëst thou not how on the brimming river

   With death he strives, where the resounding sea

Loseth its glory?'   Child of earth was never

   More swift to follow gain or loss to fly   110

   Than I hearing those words from realms for ever

Blissful descended thro' the ample sky,

   Relying on that eloquence of thine,

   Thy glory and theirs who hear its melody."

---

[7] St. Mary the Virgin, or Divine Clemency.
[8] The forlorn condition of the Poet.
[9] St. Lucy, or Illuminating Grace.
[10] This obviously refers, not to the 'stern decree' of v. 96, which is changed already, but to the 'hindrance' of v. 95.   [11] Theology.

Here ending her discourse, she bent on mine   115
   Her glowing eyes weeping, that I was made
   More eager to obey her voice divine.
And so to thee I came, and brought thee aid
   Against the fierceness of the beast that barr'd
   The readiest way o'er the fair mountain glade.   120
Why then, oh why let cowardice retard
   Thy lingering steps, nor rather entertain
   Boldness of soul meet for this labour hard—
Seeing how those three blessed ones are fain
   To care for thee within the court of heaven,   125
   And my words bid thee hope such good to attain?'
As flowerets, by the chilling breath of even
   Bow'd down and closed, their petals ope, and rear
   Upright their stems, when the sun's light is given;
So did I with my spirit's drooping cheer,   130
   Till with fresh fervour all my bosom glow'd:
   I spake as one broke free from bonds of fear;
'O she was very piteous, who bestow'd
   Her aid, and courteous thou, who did'st obey
   So soon the true words from her lips that flow'd.   135
So doth thy precious speech my fear allay,
   That all my heart is longing to fulfil
   Its first resolve this journey to essay.

Now let us go, for we have both one will.

   Thou art my guide, my lord and master thou.'   140

   So said I : then he onward moved, until

We reach'd the woody path that leads below.

CANTO III.

Per me si va.

—

ARGUMENT.

THE inscription over the gate of Hell. Dante and his Guide pass into
a region of unchanging darkness, peopled with those neutral
spirits—a vast multitude—who in their life-time had neither in-
curred infamy nor merited praise. Here they view the souls of
the lost gathering towards the river Acheron, and pressing with
eagerness into Charon's bark.

Thro' me you go to Acheron's doleful river,

  Thro' me you go to realms of endless pain,

  Thro' me you go among the lost for ever.

Eternal Justice did my being ordain :

  Power, Wisdom, Love, supreme primeval Trine,   5

  Ere yet the perishable world began,

The lofty fabric rear'd with art divine.

  With things eternal I endure eterne.

  O ye who enter, every hope resign .

In dusky colouring traced I could discern   10
   Over a gate these words ; whereat I said
   'Ah! Master, for their sense is dark and stern.'
But he as one who all my thought had read ;
   'Here must thou each misgiving leave behind,
   And every coward thought must here lie dead.   15
For we have reach'd the place where thou wilt find
   Plunged in deep woe those hapless people, who
   Have lost for aye the chief good of the mind.'
With this he put his hand in mine, and thro'
   The gloom, with cheerful face, that silenced fear,   20
   Into the hidden world my steps he drew.
Sighings, and moans, and piercing shrieks were here
   Resounding thro' the starless air beneath,
   That I upon the threshold wept to hear.
Tongues divers, speeches foul, of human breath,   25
   Each utterance of pain and wrath that telleth,
   Hoarse notes and shrill, and smiting hands therewith
A tumult made that ever eddying welleth
   Up thro' that realm in changeless gloom enshrouded,
   Like sand which the Scirocco's blast impelleth.   30
And 'Say,' I thus began with error clouded,
   'Say, Master, what tumultuous sounds amaze
   Mine ear, and who are these in sorrow shrouded ?'

Whereto he made response ; ' Here thou survey'st
   The portion of those wretched creatures, who   35
   Lived without infamy and without praise.
Mix'd are they with those worthless angels, who
   Conspired not with the rebel host, nor yet
   To God were faithful, but were self-enthrall'd.
Heaven cast them forth from its refulgent coast,   40
   Nor doth the Deep of Hell their souls receive,
   Lest spirits damn'd should have whereof to boast.'
Then I ; ' O Master, what great cause of grief
   Afflicts them, that they wail so vehemently ? '
   And he thus ; ' Briefest answer will suffice.   45
These have no hope the day of death to see,
   And their obscure existence is so base,
   They long for every other destiny.
Earth in its records hath for them no place ;
   Mercy and Justice shun their state forlorn :   50
   Speak we no more of them, but look, and pass.'
And, as I look'd, I saw an ensign borne
   Aloft, and whirling round and round—it ran
   So swiftly that all rest it seem'd to scorn.
And after it there came so long a train   55
   Of spirits that I could never have believed
   That Death so vast a multitude had slain.

Gazing till I their lineaments perceived,
   I saw the shade of him whose cowardice
   Of Peter's glorious throne himself bereaved.[1]   60
Forthwith I knew with certainty that this
   Was the vile herd of caitiff souls that were
   Hateful to God and to His enemies.
These miserable beings, that never were
   Alive, went naked, and were sorely stung   65
   By hornets and by wasps that gather'd there.
Around their faces quivering gore-drops hung,
   That mingled with their tears, and trickling o'er
   Their bodies fell disgustful worms among.
Then, bending forward further to explore,   70
   I saw much folk by a broad river's stream;
   Whereat I said; 'Master, now let thy lore
Unfold who these are, and what makes them seem
   So eager to embark those waves upon,
   As I discern by yonder fitful gleam.'   75
But he replied; 'This will appear anon,
   When we our travell'd footsteps shall have placed
   Upon the doleful shore of Acheron.'

---

[1] Pope Celestine V.

And then, with eyes in reverent awe depress'd,
   Fearing that he my questioning would blame,   80
   Up to the river I my thoughts suppress'd.

And lo! towards us o'er the wave there came
   White with his hoary hair a boatman old,
   Crying aloud, 'Woe to ye, sons of shame!

Hope not the empyreal heaven to behold: 85
   I come to bear ye to the other shore,
   Amid the eternal darkness heat and cold.

But thou, that comest ere thy life be o'er,
   Get thee away from these—for they are dead.'
   And, when he saw that I moved not the more   90

For that, 'By other paths—not here,' he said,
   'By other waters thou shalt reach the plain:
   A lighter bark must bear the living head.'

Whereto my Guide; 'Fret not thyself in vain,
   Charon, for so 'tis will'd where will and might   95
   Are one: nor seek his going to restrain.'

Then were the shaggy jaws dumb-founder'd quite
   Of the grim pilot of the livid lake,
   Who round his eyes had rings of fiery light.

But those poor weary naked souls forsake   100
   Their colour, gnashing all in furious wrath,
   Heart-stricken by the savage words he spake—

Blaspheming the Holy One of heaven—the earth
 And human kind—their sires—the time, the place,
 The seed of their begetting—and their birth.   105
And then, loud wailing all, with echoing pace
 To that accursed shore in heaps they roll,
 That waits each mortal man who spurn'd Heaven's grace.
Demonian Charon's eyes of blazing coal
 Beckon them on ; he marshals all together ;   110
 Strikes with uplifted oar each lagging soul.
As leaves, that in the drear autumnal weather
 Scatter and fall, until the umbrageous wood
 All its fair spoils unto the earth doth gather ;
Ev'n in like manner Adam's evil brood   115
 That desolate shore abandon one by one,
 As falcons by the fowler's voice pursued.
Thus are they borne across the waters dun ;
 And, ere they light upon the farther strand,
 Another crew doth muster here.   ' My son,'   120
The Master said with courteous accent bland,
 ' Those who have perish'd in the wrath of God
 Hither assemble all from every land.
And they are eager to pass o'er the flood,
 Because Heaven's justice goadeth them, till fear   125
 Is heard no more, by strong desire subdued.

No righteous spirit ever passeth here ;
   And, therefore, if with anger Charon met
   Thy coming, what his words import is clear.'
With that the dismal land beneath my feet   130
   Shook with such violence, that yet again
   The awful memory floods my limbs with sweat.
A gust of wind swept thro' the tear-sown glen ;
   Vermilion lightning flash'd along the deep,
   Bereaving me of every sense :—and then   135
I fell, as one oppress'd by sudden sleep.

CANTO IV.

Ruppemi l' alto.

—

ARGUMENT.

THE Poets descend into the first circle of Hell, or Limbo, wherein
are placed the spirits of those, who, not having sinned in the theo-
logical sense, have yet, owing to their want of baptism, come
short of salvation ; and also of those, who, having lived in
pre-Christian times, neglected the dictates of natural religion.
Emerging from the dense crowd of souls in the direction of a
light shining in the darkness, they meet the shades of Homer,
Horace, Ovid, and Lucan, by whom they are accompanied into
the separate abode of the great spirits of antiquity.

THE sleep that bound my head was broken by

A thunder peal so loud that I sprung up,

As one that is awaken'd forcibly.

Uplifted on my feet I moved around

My rested eyes, and look'd with eagerness,

To ascertain the place wherein I was.

'Tis true—upon the margin of the Abyss
 I found myself, whose caverns dolorous
 Gather the thunderous sound of agonies
Innumerable.   It was so dark, profound,   10
 And nebulous, that we on bending down
 Our steadfast gaze discern'd no single thing.
' Descend we now to the blind world below ; '
 My Teacher thus his speech all pale as death
 Began, ' I first, thou after me.'   And I,   15
Who had remark'd his pallid hue, forthwith
 Replied ; ' How shall I go, if thou dost fear,
 Whose strength alone my wavering comforteth ? '
And he return'd ; ' The anguish of the souls
 That are down here pourtrays upon my face 20
 That sympathy, which thou mistak'st for fear.
Hasten we on, for the long way doth press.'
 'Twas thus he enter'd, thus he made me enter
 The foremost circle that surrounds the Abyss.
Within, far as the listening ear could hear,   25
 No wailing sound arose, save that of sighs
 Alone, that shook the everlasting air,
Of sorrow born, without tormenting pain—
 Sorrow, that held the crowds thick-banded there
 Of infants, and of women, and of men.   30

Said the good Master then ; 'Dost thou forbear

 To ask what spirits are these that here thou seest ?

 Yet would I have thee know, ere thou draw near,

These have not sinn'd :[1] and, if they have their merits,

 'Tis not enough, for, being unbaptised,   35

 They enter'd not the portal of thy Faith :

And, if they lived before the birth of Christ,

 They render'd not due worship unto God.

 And these are they with whom my lot is cast.

For these defects—these only—we are lost,   40

 Guiltless besides : yet only in this afflicted,

 That without hope in vain desire unblest

We live.'   Great sorrow then my heart possess'd,

 Soon as I heard, because I knew that souls

 Of highest worth were in that Limbo placed.   45

And 'Tell me, O my lord—O Master, tell ;'

 Thus I began, that I might of that Faith

 Be assured, which every error doth excel ; ˷

'Went any forth from hence by his own merit,

 Or by Another's aid, who from on high   50

 Appear'd ?'   He saw my hidden drift, and made

---

[1] Sin is 'the transgression of the law,' or 'the rejection of divine grace.' The heathen, having had no divine law, and the unbaptized, lacking divine grace, had not 'sinned' in the technical theological sense of the term. This, I presume, is the meaning of the Poet.

Response, and said ; ' New in this state was I,
    When lo! to us there came One full of might,
    And on His brow the wreath of victory.
He took from us the shade of our first parent,   55
    With that of Abel, and his who 'scaped the flood,
    Moses the lawgiver obedient,
Abram the patriarch, and royal David,
    Israël, with his father, and his children,
    And Rachel, for whose sake so long he labour'd,   60
And many more; and led them up to heaven :
    And thou must know that earlier than these
    No human spirit e'er attain'd salvation.'
Not for his speaking slacken'd we our pace,
    Still thro' that dismal forest onward moving—   65
    The forest, I mean, form'd by the surging mass
Of souls. We were at no great distance from
    The highest elevation, when I saw
    A light that shone amid the encircling gloom. [2]
Onward a little farther yet in haste   70
    We went, until I could perceive in part
    That honourable people held that place.

---

[2] The light of the wisdom of the ancients shining amid the darkness
of the heathen world.

'O thou, that honourest each science and art,
   Say who are these held in such high esteem
   That from the others thus they dwell apart ? '   75
'The blaze of fame,' he forthwith made response,
   'Which sounds their praises in the world above,
   Gains grace in heaven, which thus exalteth them.'
Suddenly thro' the gloom a voice was heard ;
   'All honour to the bard of loftiest strain :   80
   His shade returns, that erst departed hence.'
Scarce had the voice its utterance ended, when
   I saw four shadows tall to us advance:
   Their looks betoken'd neither grief nor joy.
The Master then to me in brief began ;   85
   'Mark him with yonder falchion in his hand,
   Who comes before three others as their chief.
'Tis Homer, sovran poet : after him
   Horace the satirist in haste comes on :
   The third is Ovid, and the last is Lucan.   90
Because that each of them had earnèd well
   The glorious name with which they welcom'd me,
   They do me honour, and in this do well.'
Thus I beheld united the fair school
   Of that renownèd lord of loftiest song,   95
   Who soars above the rest with eagle flight.

When they awhile had held discourse among
   Themselves, to me with courteous salute
   They turn'd ; whereat the gentle Master smiled.
And greater honour yet than this they show'd   100
   To me, for of their train they made me one ;
   And I was sixth of that great company.
Thus onward to the light we paced along,
   Speaking of things now best in silence hid,
   However spoken well those scenes among.   105
Unto a lordly castle's foot we came,
   Seven times with lofty walls encompass'd round,
   Defended by a fair encircling stream.
O'er this we pass'd with ease as on dry ground :
   Thro' seven gates I enter'd with those sages :   110
   A meadow of fresh green within we found.
People were there with still and thoughtful faces ;
   Of great authority they seem'd to be,
   Speaking but seldom, with melodious voices.
We then withdrew to an open place, that lay   115
   Upon one side, lofty and fill'd with light,
   Whence we the whole surrounding scene could view.
There on the smooth enamell'd green beneath
   Were shown to me the famous spirits of old,
   Whom yet my heart exulteth to have seen.   120

There did I 'mid a numerous throng behold

   Electra, Hector, and Anchises' son,

   Cæsar all arm'd with falcon eyes ; and bold

Camilla, and the Amazonian queen

   On the other side : and there the Latin king   125

   Sitting beside Lavinia was seen.

I saw that Brutus, who expell'd Tarquin,

   Cornelia, Julia, Marcia, Lucrece ;

   Alone—apart—I saw the Saladin.

And then, when I had somewhat lifted up   130

   Mine eyes, I saw the chief of those who know,[3]

   Retired amid the philosophic crew.

Him all admire, all give him honour due :

   And nearer to him standing than the rest

   Plato and Socrates appear'd : he too   135

Who builds the world on chance, Democritus;

   Diogenes, Anaxagoras, and Thales,

   Zeno, Empedocles, and Heraclitus ;

And he, of herbs who track'd the qualities,

   Dioscorides. Orpheus too was there,   140

   Tully, and Linus, moral Seneca,

Geometrician Euclid, Ptolemy,

   Galen, Hippocrates, and Avicenna,

   And he who made the famous commentary,

Averrois.—I cannot all retrace, 145
   So hurried onward by the exhaustless theme
   That oft-times words with things cannot keep pace.
Our company of six divided here :
   Another way I went with my sage Guide
   Forth from the tranquil to the troubled air ; 150
And came into a part where is no light.

---

  ^² Aristotle. I am indebted to Cary's translation for the expression 'thunderous sound' in v. 9 of this Canto.

CANTO V.

Cosi discesi.

—

ARGUMENT.

DANTE and his Guide pass into the second circle, in which they
view the souls of Carnal Sinners, in utter darkness—the sport and
prey of racking whirlwinds. Dante converses with Francesca and
Paolo Malatesta, from the former of whom he hears the narrative
of their disastrous love.

THUS downward from the foremost circle I went
  Into the second, that lesser space surroundeth,
  And greater pain, which goads to loud lament.
There with his grin terrific Minos standeth,
  Examineth offences at the gate,   5
  Judgeth, and doometh, as himself he windeth.
For when the spirit born with evil fate
  Before him comes, it maketh full confession
  And that dread Punisher inquireth straight
What place in Hell befitteth its transgression;   10
  Then girds him with his tail so oft as will
  Denote the grade ordain'd for its dismission.

D

Always before him many stand : they go,

    Each in his turn, and one by one, to judgment :

    They speak, and hear, and then are hurl'd below.   15

' O thou that comest to this house of sorrow,'

    Cried Minos unto me, when he beheld me,

    Leaving the business of that dreadful office ;

' See how thou enterest, and on what reliest :

    Be not deceived by the broad entrance way.'   20

    To whom the Master ; ' Wherefore vainly criest ?

It lieth not with thee his course to stay.

    'Tis thus by fate decreed, and will'd where power

    Effectuates will : forbear ; and ask no more.'

Thereon the notes of woe began to sound   25

    Nearer and yet more near, till we alight

    There where loud anguish smites upon the ear.

I found me in a place void of all light,

    That moaneth as the troubled ocean moaneth,

    When roused in conflict with the tempest's might.   30

The infernal hurricane, that never resteth,

    Gathers the spirits in its swift career,

    And turns about and drives them where it listeth.

When yawns the precipice before their eyes,

    Shrieks, moans, and lamentations rend the air,   35

    And blasphemies against the heavenly Power.

I understood that to this torment dire
   The souls of carnal sinners were condemn'd,
   Whose rebel wills rejected reason's lore.
And like as starlings, on their wings upborne,   40
   Large flocks together in the wintry season,
   So by that blast were those ill spirits borne
This way and that, now up, now downward driven :
   Nor any hope their wretchedness allays
   Or of repose, or of less grievous pain :   45
And like as cranes chanting their dolorous lays
   Drift thro' the air in far extending train;
   So came they uttering long drawn wailings drear—
Those shadows urged by the wild hurricane :
   Whereat I said ; ' O Master, who are these   50
   Spirits whom the black whirlwind scourges thus ? '
And he then said to me ; ' The first of these,
   Of whom thou seekest to have knowledge, held
   Imperial sway o'er many languages.
She was so lapsed in lawless wantonness,   55
   All lust she licensed by her laws, in faith
   Thus to remove the shame wherein she was—
Semiramis, of whom the legend saith
   That she gave suck to Ninus, and was his spouse :
   She held the land which now the Sultan swayeth.   60

Next cometh one by hapless love self-slain—
    She, who broke faith with the ashes of Sichæus : [1]
    Cleopatra next to her, luxurious dame.'
Helen I saw, for whom so many years
    Of wasteful strife prevail'd ; and great Achilles,   65
    Who join'd the fray at last, by love [2] impell'd.
Paris was there, and Tristan ; . . . . and the place
    Was rife with hundreds more—by him then named
    And shown to me—whom love bereft of life.
Thus having heard the experienced Guide recount   70
    By name the knights and dames of ancient time,
    My grief o'ercame me, and I almost swoon'd.
At length I spake thus ; ' Poet, I would fain
    Converse with yonder pair, [3] who come together,
    And seem to float so lightly on the air.'   75
Whereto he thus replied ; ' Watch thou, till they
    Approach nearer to us : then summon them
    By that love which is theirs, and they will come.'
Soon as the wind bore them to where we stood,
    I lifted up my voice ; ' O wearied ones,   80
    Come hither, and speak with us, if nought forbids.'

---

[1] Dido.   [2] His love for Patroclus.
[3] Francesca and Paolo Malatesta.

Then, as two doves that by desire call'd
  With moveless wings outspread to their sweet nest
  Float thro' the air by longing hearts impell'd ;
Forth from the crowd where Dido was they pass'd,   85
  They came to us thro' the dun air malign,
  So vehement was my passionate cry.   And thus
One spake ; ' O being gracious and benign,
  Who comest thro' the black wind visiting
  Us, who by violent hands erewhile were slain ;   90
Were He our friend, who sways the universe,
  We would beseech Him for thy peace, who thus
  Pitiest our evil plight, and wills perverse.
And seeing thou would'st hold discourse with us,
  We too will listen and converse with thee,   95
  While the fierce whirlwind keepeth silence thus.
The land where I was born lies by the sea,
  That gleams along that coast, where Po descends,
  To have repose with his attendant streams.
Love, that in gentle heart soon glows, o'ercame   100
  Him for that beauty which was reft from me
  So foully that the anguish yet remains.
Love, that to none beloved remitteth love's
  Return, seized me for his enchanting self
  So strongly that it still lingers as thou seest.   105

Love brought us to one grave : the lowest hell

   Awaiteth him by whom our lives were sped.'

   Such was the utterance from her lips that fell.

At hearing which from those woe-wearied souls,

   I bow'd my head, and held it down so long   110

   That the Bard said to me ; 'What ponderest thou ?'

After some pause, I thus began ; 'Alas!

   What yearnings, and what blissful reveries

   Impell'd them to that lamentable pass !'

And then I turn'd to them, and thus again   115

   My speech renewed ; 'Francesca, thy afflictions

   Bring tears of grief and pity to mine eyes.

But tell me—at the time of those sweet sighs

   How happen'd it that Love enabled you

   Each other's dubious wish to recognise ?'   120

And she replied ; 'There is no greater sorrow

   Than recollecting times of happiness

   In misery : and this thy Teacher⁴ knows.

But if thou hast so great desire to know

   How that entrancing love began to sway   125

   Our hearts, I will repeat the tale of woe.

---

⁴ Boëthius. 'In omni adversitate fortunæ infelicissimum genus infortunii est fuisse felicem et non esse.' *De Consolatione.* L. ii. pr. 4.

We chanced to read for our delight one day

   Of Lancelot, how love enthrallèd him :

   Alone we read, all unsuspectingly.

And many times that tale our eyes made dim   130

   With tears, and paled our cheeks ; but 'twas one place

   Alone that vanquish'd us : for when we came

To where it was narrated how that fair

   Enchanting face was kiss'd by one so fond,

   So dear, he, who from me will never be   135

Dissever'd, kiss'd my lips all tremblingly.

   The book, the writer served as Galahad [5]

   For us.   We read therein no more that day.'

Thus while one spirit spake, the other stay'd

   Speechless, but moan'd, and wept.   I at that tale   140

   Of sorrow swoon'd, and was as one half dead ;

And, as a corpse falls, to the ground I fell.

---

[5] Galahad was the name of the person who acted as go-between to Guinevere and Lancelot.

CANTO VI.

Al tornar della mente.

—

ARGUMENT.

THE Poets enter the third circle, where, under a ceaseless tempest of
rain, hail, and snow, the souls of the Gluttonous are tormented by
Cerberus. Dante here converses with Ciacco, a Florentine, who
predicts the expulsion of the Neri from Florence, and their return
within three years. Dante inquires whether the torments of the
lost will be increased or diminished after the day of judgment. In
reply Virgil refers him to the maxim of Aristotle, that beings are
more or less sensible of good and evil in proportion as they have
attained a greater or less degree of perfection. After the judgment
the lost will recover their bodies, and will thus, in accordance with
this maxim, experience an increase of suffering. On the descent
towards the fourth circle they find Plutus—the arch-enemy.

WHEN life and sense return'd, erewhile suspended
  In presence of the kindred shades, whose anguish
  Shrouded me all in dazing mist of sorrow,
New torments I behold, and new tormented
  Spirits around me strown, where'er I move,   5
  Where'er I turn, or bend my wistful gaze.

I found myself in the third circle, where

    The accursed everlasting showers descend

    Baleful and cold—unchanging evermore

In rule and quality. Large hail and snow   10

    And ink-black rain pours thro' the darken'd air:

    The foul earth stinks whereon that deluge falls.

The savage-hearted monster multiform,

    Cerberus, with his three throats dog-like bayeth

    Over the people that are whelmèd thus.   15

Eyes fiery red—black matted beard beneath

    His visage grim—huge paunch—and talon'd hands—

    He flays the souls, and tears them limb from limb.

They howl like dogs beneath the drenching rain,

    With one side making shelter for the other,   20

    And shifting oft—those hapless spirits profane.

When Cerberus, the great worm, us descried,

    He open'd wide his mouths, and show'd his fangs,

    And shook in every limb : whereat my Guide

Stooping forthwith stretch'd out his hands, and took   25

    Of that foul earth, and flung whole handfuls down

    Those ravenous throats. As when a dog with pangs

Of hunger yelps and howls, but ceaseth soon,

    When he has seized his prey, and ravening gloats

    Over the wish'd-for meal, intent thereon ;   30

So brought to silence were the three foul throats

   Of demon Cerberus, who dins alway

   The souls until they fain would lose the sense

Of hearing. Onward o'er the spirits, that lay

   Prostrate beneath the rain, we went, and placed   35

   Our steps on shadowy forms that substance seem'd.

They lay diffused upon the ground—all who

   Were there, save one, who raised himself to sit,

   When he beheld us passing near. 'Thou who

Art borne thro' this infernal pit,' he said   40

   To me, 'bethink thee who I am, if yet

   Thou can'st. Thy life began ere mine was sped.'

And I replied ; 'Perhaps it is thy state

   Of agony withdraws thee from my mind

   So that it seemeth that I never saw thee.   45

But tell me who thou art, that in this blind

   Abode art placed, and with such pain that, if

   There be more grievous, none hath more distaste.'

And he replied ; 'Thy city, [1] which is rife

   With envy so that it hath now excell'd   50

   All bounds, possess'd me in the light of life.

---

[1] Florence, divided into the factions of the Bianchi, to which the
Poet belonged, and the Neri.

By you, my townsmen, I was Ciacco[2] call'd.

    For the wide-wasting vice of gluttony

    I welter, as thou seest, beneath the rain :

Nor is it thus with me alone, but all   55

    These hapless souls unto like pain are doom'd

    For like offence.'   He ended here, and I

Thus made response ; ' Ciacco, thy troublous state

    Afflicts me so that I am moved to tears.

    But tell me, if thou knowest, whereunto   60

The citizens of the divided state

    Will come ; if any there be just ; and say

    Whence grew this factious spirit to such height ? '

And he replied ; ' After long struggle they

    Will come to bloodshed, when the forest party[3]   65

    Will with outrageous violence expel

The other[4]—destin'd soon itself to fall

    Within three years, and see the other rise

    Again with help of one who some while steers

A middle course.[5]   Long time the victor bears   70

    His head on high, weighing with heavy hand

    Upon the foe, who chafes resentfully.

---

[2] Ciacco is described by Landino as ' un uomo pieno d'urbanità e di motti e di facezie e di soavissima conversazione.'   A gloss adds that he was 'homo de curiâ gulosus valdè.'

[3] The Bianchi.   [4] The Neri.   [5] Between the two factions, siding

There are two just men [6] there, who live defamed

   And hated.   Envy, pride, and avarice

   Are the three sparks that have men's hearts inflamed.' 75

With that he from his mournful strain surceased.

   And I resumed; 'Yet would I further learn

   Of thee, and crave the gift of further speech.

Of Farinata, and Tegghiaio, who

   So worthy were; of Jacob Rusticucci,   80

   Arrigo, Mosca, and the others, who

To do well enter'd fair; [7]—say in what place

   They dwell, for I have great desire to know

   If they are lapt in bliss, or lost in Hell.'

And he replied; 'Whelm'd in the deep below   85

   Are they with blacker souls for heavier guilt;

   As thou descending to that deep wilt know.

---

with neither.   This is Buti's interpretation of the words 'che teste piaggia,' which he refers to Pope Boniface VIII., who brought about the expulsion of the Bianchi by the instrumentality of Charles de Valois.

[6] It is not known who these are. Sigr. Bianchi thinks they may have been Dante himself, and Guido Cavalcanti, mentioned in Canto x., who is described by Benvenuto da Imola as 'Alter oculus Florentiæ tempore Dantis.'

[7] These persons (with the exception of Arrigo Fifanti, who is not mentioned elsewhere) are introduced later in the poem; Farinata degli Uberti in the 10th, Tegghiaio Aldobrandi degli Adimari, and Jacob Rusticucci in the 16th, and Mosca degli Uberti (or, as some think, dei Lamberti) in the 28th, Canto.

But, when thou shalt be in the joyous world,

   Make me to dwell in others' memory :

   Ask now no more, for I no more will tell.'   90

This said, his fix'd eyes all askance he roll'd ;

   A moment look'd at me ; then bow'd his head,

   And with the other nighted spirits fell.

When thus my Guide ; ' From yonder couch they rise

   No more until the angel-trump shall sound.   95

   Then, when the Adversary Power shall come,

Each one will to the cheerless tomb repair,

   His former shape and moulder'd flesh resume,

   And hear the aye-resounding voice of doom.'

Onward with slow steps o'er the loathsome mass   100

   Of rain and spirits blent we held our way,

   Touching a little on the life to come.

Whence I inquired ; ' O Master, say, these torments—

   Will they increase after the general doom,

   Or will they be as now, or less intense ?'   105

Whereto he said ; ' To thy science [8] repair,

   Which wills that as each thing more perfect is,

   It has a keener sense of joy and woe.

Albeit this accursed people ne'er

   Attaineth unto full perfection, yet   110

   Will they be nearer to it then than now.' [9]

Thus round that circling road we wound our way,
    Conversing more than I can here repeat :
    We gain'd the pathway that conducts below :
There found we Plutus,[10] the arch-enemy.   115

---

[8] The Aristotelian philosophy. Metaph. iv. 16.
[9] The inference—that on recovering their bodies they will experience an increase of suffering—is implied.
[10] The God of riches.

CANTO VII.

Pape Satan.

—

ARGUMENT.

THE Poets descend into the fourth circle. Here they view the souls of
the Avaricious and of the Prodigal, in large troops, arranged in
circles, and rolling heavy weights, which they dash against one
another. The Prodigal taunt the Avaricious with their miser-
liness, and the Avaricious taunt the Prodigal with their reckless
expenditure. Driven asunder, they retrace their steps, each pur-
suing the course of his own semi-circle, until they reach the ex-
treme point, where they are again severed. Conversing on the
office of Fortune, and the vicissitudes of which she is the author,
the Poets descend into the fifth circle, following the course of a
rivulet which brings them to the margin of Styx ;—where, wallow-
ing on the surface of its filthy waters, they view the souls of the
Angry, smiting and rending one another in ferocious conflict.
From beneath they catch the echoes of the inarticulate wailings
of the Slothful, who are fixed in the slime at the bottom of the
pool. Having made a wide circuit round the edge of the lake,
they arrive at the base of a tower.

' PAPE Satan, Pape Satan, aleppe ! '

Plutus 'gan bay with hideous din—but he,

The gentle-hearted sage who all things knew,

---

[1] This line is said to mean, ' Ho ! Satan, ho ! Satan, my chief ! '
' Pape,' is probably the Greek παπαί. ' Aleppe ' is Hebrew.

Spake word of comfort ; ' Let not thy dismay
    Confound thee : whatsoe'er his power, it shall   5
    Not stay thy progress down this rock-hewn way.'
Then rounding swift upon that passion-blown
    Visage, he said ; ' Accursed wolf, be still !
    Within thyself that rabid wrath consume.
Not without cause is this descent into   10
    The gulf : 'tis will'd on high, where Michael pour'd
    Vengeance upon the Heaven-revolted crew.'
As when a ship's sails swollen by the gale
    Collapse and fall about the shivering mast ;
    So to the earth the savage monster fell.   15
Thus down into the fourth abyss we pass'd,
    Traversing more of that dark region fill'd
    With all the evils of the universe.
Ah me ! Justice Divine—how dost thou heap
    New pains and travails, which these eyes beheld :   20
    Ah ! wherefore take such vengeance on our sin ?
As wave with wave upon Charybdis' pool
    Meets, and is broken, and runs diverse ; so
    The people here in eddying circles move.
Here saw I folk more numerous than elsewhere   25
    Thronging on either side with clamorous howls,
    And rolling by main force huge weights along.

Encountering, they dash together ; and then

    Each one forthwith wheels round, and backward rolls,

    Crying aloud ; 'Why hoard ye ?' and 'Why d'ye spend?' 30

Thus they return along the gloomy ring,

    Each in his place to the opposing point,

    Crying always in their opprobrious strain.

Then each one, after shock, wheels round again,

    Thro' his half-circle, for another tilt. 35

    I, all my heart thrill'd thro' with anguish keen,

Said ; ' O my Master, now to me impart

    What spirits are these, and if they all were priests—

    These with the shaven crowns upon our left.'

And he replied ; ' All these in their first lives 40

    Were so warped in their mental sight that they

    In their expense no fitting measure kept—

Distinguish'd clearly by their piercing cries

    When to those two points of the ring they come,

    Where the conflicting faults drive them apart. 45

These without covering of hair upon

    Their crowns were priests and Popes and Cardinals,

    In whom the excess of avarice was found.'

Then I ; ' O Master, surely amongst all these

    There needs must be whom I can recognise— 50

    Souls that were tainted by those ills.' But he

E

Made answer thus ; ' Vainly thou dost surmise :
   The ingloriousness wherein their lives were spent
   Makes it impossible to recognise
Their lineaments.   They will for ever come   55
   To the two shocks : these from the tomb will rise
   With clenchèd fist, and these with hair all cropt. [2]
Spending and hoarding ill hath reft from them
   The beauteous world, and set them in this strife.
   How drear it is no words could e'er unfold.   60
Now may'st thou learn, my son, of how short life
   Those good things are, which Fortune doth control ;
   For which mankind wageth perpetual strife.
For all the gold beneath the moon, and all
   That ever was, for these poor weary souls   65
   Could never gain one moment of repose.'
' Master,' I said, ' be pleased also to unfold
   To me—this Fortune—who she is, by whom
   The good things of the world are thus controll'd ?'
And he replied ; ' O foolish creatures ! how   70
   Great is that ignorance which doth enfold
   Your minds ! now to my words give heed.—He whose

---

[2] The clenched fist denotes avarice ; cropt hair prodigality, which squanders everything, 'fino ai capelli,' *i.e.*, 'even to the hair,' as the Italians say.

Omniscience all else transcends, who made

 The heavens, and gave them Angels ministrant—

 So that each part to each part glory lends—   75

Distributing with equal hand the light ;

 So for the glories of this world He hath

 Ordain'd a general Minister and Guide,

To shift from time to time earth's fleeting toys

 From race to race, from house to house, beyond   80

 The feeble shifts which human sense employs.

Thus one race waxeth strong, another weak,

 Following the guidance of her hand, which works

 In secret, as within the grass the snake.

Your knowledge cannot vie with hers : she all   85

 Events foreseeing orders each, and rules

 Her kingdom, as the other Angels theirs.

Her work no rest or intermission knows ;

 Necessity compels her to be swift :

 So many are they whom sudden change o'erthrows.   90

'Tis she who is so often put to shame

 Even by those who ought to give her praise,

 Giving wrongful reproach, and evil fame.

But she hears not, and in the realms of bliss,

 Amid the other primal creatures, rolls   95

 Her sphere, rejoicing in her blessedness.

Descend we now to lower depths of woe.

    Now falls each star that rose when we began

    Our course : nor may we linger here.'—Across

The circle then we went to the other side,   100

    Hard by a fountain, which springs there, and pours

    Down a slope channel from itself derived.

Gloomy and dark those waters were—more dark

    Than purple : we with them found entrance soon

    Into a pathway strange, that downward bore   105

Our steps towards a lake, whose name is Styx,

    Form'd by this rueful streamlet when it gains

    The bottom of those black malignant plains.

And, as I stood to view the scene, I saw

    Much people rolling on that putrid flood,   110

    Slime-spatter'd, naked, and with furious mien.

These in their rage not with their hands alone

    But with head breast and feet each other struck,

    And tore themselves in pieces with their fangs.

My Guide then spake ; ' Here, O my son, thou seest   115

    The spirits of those whom anger overcame :

    And I would have thee know for certain that

Beneath this water there are souls whose sighing

    Makes heave the bubbling surface, as thou seest,

    Where'er the eye roves round.' And thus they sung— 120

Those spirits mire-ingulf'd ; ' All gloom were we
   In the sweet air illumin'd by the sun,
   Stifling our souls within with slothful fumes ;
Now we have gloom in the black pool undone.'
   This they repeat with gurgling sound within   125
   Their throats, but words complete can utter none.
Thus long way round that loathsome pool, between
   The dry bank and the waves, in haste we wound
   Our course, with eyes down cast on those who filth
Ingorged : we came to a tower's base at last.   130

CANTO VIII.

Io dico seguitando.

ARGUMENT.

THE Poets had noticed two beacon lights at the top of the tower. These denoted the arrival of two souls. There was also a third light on the other side of the lake. This announced the approach of the Ferryman. A boat arrives in charge of Phlegyas, who in his life-time had burnt the temple of Apollo, and whose function it now was to convey the souls of heretics into the fiery City of Dis. On the passage Dante encounters, and converses with, Philippo Argenti, a Florentine, who had been noted for his brutal and ferocious temper. Passing within the moats which surround the territory of Dis, they find the gate thronged with devils, who resist their entrance. Excluded by the devils, they await the advent of aid from above.

My theme pursuing, I relate that some
 Time ere we gain'd the lofty turret's base
 Our eyes roved upward towards the summit, where
We saw two little streams of light extend,
 To which a third made answer from afar—   5
 So far that it was scarce discernible.

Then turning to that other sea, wherein
 All wisdom lay, I said ; ' What meaneth this ?
 What answereth yon flamelet ? and who are they
That tend it ?' He replied ; ' Over the dun   10
 Waters already may'st thou note what comes
 Apace, if the lake-fumes conceal it not.'
Ne'er leapt the winged arrow from the string
 Or ran its course more swiftly thro' the air
 Than I descried a little vessel there   15
Shoot o'er the leaden waves to where we stood,
 Under the guidance of a single pilot,
 Who cried aloud, ' Ho art thou come—damn'd spirit ! '
To whom the Master spake ; ' Phlegyas ! Phlegyas !
 In vain thou criest thus—this time : thou wilt 20
 Not have us save in passing o'er the lake.'
As one who hears of some great wrong that hath
 Been done to him, then chafes resentfully ;
 So was't with Phlegyas in his gather'd wrath.
Thereon my Guide went down into the boat, 25
 And then he made me enter after him,
 Nor, till I was within it, seem'd it fraught.
Scarce had the Guide and I made entrance, when
 The ancient craft went ploughing thro' the water
 More deeply than with others it was wont. 30

While thus we sped across the stagnant pool,
    One cover'd o'er with slime arose, and said
    To me ; ' Why comest thou before the time ? '
And I replied ; ' I come, but not to stay :
    But who art thou made thus deform ? ' and he ;   35
    ' Thou seëst I am one of those in pain.'
I answer'd swift ; ' With wailing and with tears,
    Accursed spirit ! may'st thou e'er remain :
    I know thee yet, all grimèd as thou art.'
Then towards the bark he stretch'd out both his hands ; 40
    Whereat the Master caught and thrust him back,
    Saying, ' Away there with the other hounds ! '
And then around my neck his arms he flung,
    And kiss'd my cheek, and said ; ' Disdainful soul !
    Thrice blessed was the womb that compass'd thee.   45
He was full fraught with pride in the fair world,
    With naught of grace to deck his memory ;
    Thus is his spirit rack'd with furious rage.
How many, that once held themselves on high,
    Wallow like swine impure, view'd thro' all time   50
    With hate, and scorn, and shameful ignominy ! '
Then I ; ' Master, it would rejoice my soul
    To see him soused within this bestial slush,
    Ere we alight from off the pool.'   And he

Responded thus; 'Or ere the other shore   55
   Comes within prospect, thou shalt have thy wish.
   'Tis meet thou should'st have joy of this desire.'
After a while I saw so fierce a rush
   Made at him by his fellows in the mire,
   That still I bless and praise my God.   They all   60
Cried with one voice; 'At Philip Argentine!' [1]
   The fierce Florentine spirit in his wrath
   Turn'd round, and with his talons rent his flesh.
Here left we him that I no more can tell:
   But to mine ears loud cries of anguish borne   65
   Made me bend forward opening wide mine eyes.
When the good Master thus; 'Here, O my son,
   The city which is called Dis draws near,
   With its dread citizens, a numerous throng.'
And I; 'O Master, in the valley there   70
   Clearly I can discern its minarets
   Vermilion-hued, as tho' with circling fire
Impaled.'   And he replied; 'The eternal flame,
   That glows within, imparts this ruddy hue,
   As thou beholdest in this nether hell.'   75

---

[1] So called from having his horse shod with silver.

We pass'd within the deep wide moats, with which
    That melancholy land is compass'd round,
    The walls thereof seem'd built of gleaming steel.
Not without first wide circuit made we came
    Unto a place where with loud voice the pilot   80
    ' Out with you !' cried to us, ' the gate is here.'
More than a thousand thronging there I saw—
    Spirits rain'd down from heaven—who were saying
    Wrathfully ; ' Who is this that comes within
The region of the dead by death unslain ?'   85
    Whereat the experienced Master made a sign
    Of wish to speak with them apart : and then
They bated somewhat of their huge disdain,
    And said ; ' Come thou alone : let him depart,
    Who thus hath dared to enter this domain.   90
On his fool's road let him return alone,
    If so he can : but thou shalt here remain—
    Thou who hast borne him thro' this land of gloom.'
Think, reader, how my courage falter'd then,
    Hearing the sound of those accursed words :   95
    I thought that I should ne'er return again.
' O my beloved Guide, who more than seven
    Times hast restored my safety, and hast led
    My steps thro' perils dire that round me lay,

Leave me not here all comfortless,' I said   100

   ' And if our further progress be forbidden,

   Let us with speed retrace our steps together.'

But the good Master who had led me thither

   Made answer thus ; ' Thy fear dismiss, for none

   Can stay our onward course : 'tis will'd by Heaven.   105

Attend me here, and be thy weary spirit

   By the sweet influence of hope sustain'd

   And cheer'd, for in this nether world I ne'er

Will leave thee.'   Thus he went ; and I remain'd

   In doubt, by the sweet sire abandon'd there,   110

   With yea and nay contending in my brain.

I could not hear the words he spake ; but they

   Had not been long in conference, before

   Each one ran back to try the chance of fight.

Then did those adversaries close the door   115

   In the face of my lord, who stay'd without,

   And back to me return'd with slacken'd pace—

His eyes upon the ground, his brow bereft

   Of all its confidence, while thus with sighs

   He spake ; ' Who hath to me denied the house   120

Of woe ?'   Then to me turning ; ' Be not thou

   Dismay'd at my distress, for we shall win,

   Whate'er defences are prepared within.

This insolence of theirs is nothing new ;

   'Twas shown before at the less secret gate,   125

   Which yet remains unbarr'd.   'Twas there thou saw'st

The unearthly scroll ; already nigh at hand

   'Twixt us and it across the steep comes down,

   Passing the circles without escort, One

Whose might will open yet the doleful land.'   130

CANTO IX.

Quel color che vilta.

—

THE ARGUMENT.

DANTE, alarmed at the language in which his Guide, after expressing
his confidence in their ultimate triumph over the devils, suggested
for a moment the opposite alternative, enquires whether the spirits
in Limbo ever descended into the lower circles of Hell. To.
this Virgil replies that he had himself been made to descend to
the very lowest depth by Erictho, the Thessalian sorceress. The
conversation is here interrupted by the apparition of the Furies.
A terrific sound—as of a rushing mighty wind—announces the
advent of the Angel, who opens the gate of the City. Within
they find a wide territory, overspread with burning tombs, con-
taining the Heresiarchs and their followers.

THAT hue which coward fear upon my cheek

　　Then traced, when I beheld my Guide return,

　　His own unwonted pallor soon repress'd.

Moveless he stood as one intent to hear ;

　　For sight was powerless to conduct him far　　5

　　Thro' the dense mist and thro' the dusky air.

' Nathless it shall be ours to win this fight,'

　　He thus began ; ' if not . . . . our help is sure.

　　Ah me ! why tarries yet that other one ?'

I noticed how he cover'd o'er the doubt　　　　　　10

　　At first express'd, and that his after-thought

　　Was different from that which went before.

Yet none the less my fear was strengthen'd by

　　His interrupted speech, wherein perhaps

　　I found a ghastlier import than he meant.　　15

' Into this deep of the Abyss descends

　　Any from the first sphere, wherein is found

　　No pain beyond the loss of hope ?'　I this

Inquiry made, and he then made response ;

　　' It seldom comes to pass that one of us　　20

　　Maketh this journey whereon we are bound.

'Tis true that once before I was conjured

Down here by that fierce Erito, [1] who call'd

　　The shades back to their bodies.　I had been

But short time of the flesh despoil'd, when she　25

　　Made me to pass thro' yonder wall, to raise

　　A spirit from the sphere where Judas lies.

That is the lowest place, and most obscure,

　　And furthest from the heaven that circleth all. [2]

　　I know the road ; therefore rest thou secure.　　30

This lake, which breathes the baleful stench around,

    Girds with its sullen flow the doleful city,

    Where none can enter without wrath.' And more

Than this he spake, which I could not retain,

    Because mine eyes were now drawn wholly towards   35

    The blazing summit of the tower, whereon

Appear'd uplifted suddenly the three

    Infernal Furies, smear'd with blood, who seem'd

    Women in shape and gesture—girded round

With hydras all of greenest hue, and curl'd   40

    About their angry brows with cerasts horn'd

    And serpents thick entwined.—And he, who knew

Full well the ministers of her who sways

    The realm of everlasting wailings, said

    To me ; 'Behold the fell Erinnyes !   45

Here on the left hand is Megæra : there

    Wailing upon the right Alecto drear :

    Midst is Tisiphone.' And then he ceased.

Their talons rent their breasts ; and with their palms

    They smote each other, and exclaim'd so loud,   50

    That I in terror to the Poet clung.

---

[1] Or Erictho, a Thessalian sorceress, referred to by Lucan. Phars. vi. 589.

[2] The Primum Mobile, the outermost of the heavenly spheres.

'Change him to adamant—Medusa!' thus

    They all exclaim'd with eyes bent downward; 'so

    Shall we revenge the assault which Theseus made.'[s]

'Turn thee behind, and close thine eyes, for if   55

    The Gorgon once appear, and thou behold,

    For thee will be no journeying up to light.'

So spake my Guide, nor rested there, but turn'd

    Me round himself, nor on my hands relied,

    But with his own mine eyelids held fast shut.   60

O ye, that have discerning minds, behold

    And meditate the hidden sense involved

    Under the covering of the mystic verse.

And now far echoing o'er the troubled waves

    Broke the loud crash of a terrific sound   65

    That shook both margins of the lake, and seem'd

As if occasion'd by a wind that, lash'd

    Into strong fury by conflicting heat,

    Heedless of all restraint the forest cleaves,

The boughs rends down, and strews them all abroad :   70

    Wrapt in a cloud of dust it tears along ;

    The wild beasts and the shepherds fly dismay'd.

---

[s] Theseus aided Pirithous in his attempt to carry off Proserpine.

Mine eyes he loosed, and ' Now,' said he, ' direct
   The visual nerve athwart the eternal foam,
   On this side where the smoke is most intense.'   75
As frogs in presence of the water-snake,
   Their foe, fly frighted, shoaling thro' the waves,
   Till 'neath the sheltering mould they vanish all ;
More than a thousand ruin'd spirits there
   I saw thus flying before One, who pass'd   80
   Across the Stygian pool with feet unwet.
He brush'd the clammy dew from off his face,
   His left hand often passing o'er his brow ;
   Nor gave he other sign of weariness.
I could perceive that he was sent from heaven,   85
   And moved towards my Guide, who signall'd me
   To hold my peace, and do him reverence.
Ah me ! how full of high disdain he seem'd !
   He came up to the gate, which with his wand
   He open'd, for no bars could him restrain.   90
' Outcasts of heaven, despisèd people ! ' thus
   Upon the horrid threshold he began ;
   'Whence harbour ye this insolence within
Your breasts ?   Ah ! wherefore kick ye against that will
   Which never can be frustrate of its ends,   95
   And which has oft before your pains increased ?

What boots it thus to wrestle with the fates ?

   Your Cerberus —if ye remember—still

   Weareth for this his chin and dewlap flay'd.'

Then back upon the filthy road he turn'd,   100

   And made no sign to us, but seem'd as one

   Whom other and more urgent care corrodes

Than of the work whereon to us he came.

   And we our steps moved onward towards the land

   In peace after the hallow'd words.   Within   105

The gates we pass'd without annoy ; and I,

   Who had a longing wish to know the state

   Within those walls inclosed, soon as I found

Myself within, moved round mine eyes, and lo !

   On either hand I saw a spacious plain   110

   Tormented all with agonising woe.

Ev'n as at Arles, where the Rhone stays its flow,

   Ev'n as at Pola, where Quarnaro bounds

   The Italian land, and laves its frontier,

The sepulchres make all the strand to heave   115

   In mounds ; so did they here on either hand,

   Save that the scene was far more dread : for here

There were dispread between the sepulchres

   Careering fires, from which accrued such heat

   That iron for the founder's use requires   120

None greater: and from beneath their lids—which were
   Suspended—issued forth such doleful cries
   As witness'd the abode of tortured souls. [4]
When I thus; 'Master, say, what spirits are these
   That buried thus within these vaults disclose   125
   Their presence by these lamentable sighs?'
And he thereto; 'Here are the Heresiarchs
   With their adherents of each sect, and far
   More than thou would'st believe the tombs contain.
Like here with like lie sepulchred for ever: 130
   And different temperatures are found within.'
He therewith moving towards the right, we pass'd
Between the torments and the lofty walls.

---

[4] The sepulchres referred to in this passage are probably old Roman tombs. The Rhone forms a lake at Arles. Quarnaro is the gulf of that name, which washes the confines of Italy and Croatia.

CANTO X.

Ora sen va.

ARGUMENT.

THE Poets traverse the City of Dis. Dante converses with Farinata
degli Uberti, the Ghibelline chief; also with Cavalcante Cavalcanti,
a Florentine of the Guelf party, whose son, Guido, was his friend.

THUS while we paced along a narrow way
    Between the land's wall and the torturing fires,
    My Master first, and I close following him,
' Virtue supreme, who thro' the unhallow'd spheres
    Leadest me as thou willest,' I began ;   5
    ' Speak to me, and my longing wish fulfil.
The spirits couch'd within the sepulchres—
    Can they be seen ?   For I perceive that all
    The lids are raised, and no one keepeth watch.'
And he replied ; ' They all will be fast shut   10
    When from Jehoshaphat their inmates shall
    Return revested with the bodies which

They left above.[1]   On this side lie interr'd,

 With Epicurus and his followers, all

 Who with the body make the soul to die.   15

Touching the question which thou askest me,

 Within here thou shalt soon be satisfied :

 So shall that wish which thou unfoldest not.'[2]

Whence I replied ; ' I do not keep conceal'd

 My thought from thee, kind Guide, save that I may 20

 Speak little, as thou oft hast warnèd me.'

' Tuscan, who thro' the fiery city thus

 Rovest alive such sweet speech uttering,

 O stay thy course, and rest awhile with us.

That voice of thine declareth thee to be   25

 A native of that noble land wherein

 I wrought perhaps with a too troublous hand.'

Suddenly from among the sepulchres

 Issued this utterance, whereat I clung

 In fear somewhat more closely to my Guide ; 30

Who said to me ; ' Turn thee : what doest thou ?

 See ! see ! where Farinata stands upright :

 From the waist upward thou may'st him behold.'

---

[1] That is, after the day of judgment. ' I will gather all nations, and will bring them down into the valley of Jehoshaphat, and will plead with them there.' Joel iii. 2. See also Inf. vi. 95 ; xiii. 103.

[2] Probably the wish to see Farinata, already mentioned in Canto vi.

I had already fix'd my gaze on him ;
    And he appear'd with breast and brow uprear'd,   35
    As holding Hell itself in high disdain.
Promptly and resolutely the Master then
    Thrust me between the sepulchres to him ;
    And thus he added ; ' Let thy speech be plain.'
Soon as I came before his tomb, a while   40
    At me he gazed, and then with lips of scorn
    Demanded thus ; ' What ancestry was thine ? '
I, who was all desirous to obey,
    Conceal'd them not, but straight unfolded all ;
    Whence he his eye-brows somewhat raised, and then   45
Forthwith made answer ; ' Fiercely opposed were they
    To me, and to my kith, and to my party : [3]
    Once and again I drave them forth ! '   ' If they
Were driven forth, yet did they from all parts
    Return,' I answer'd swift, ' once and again !   50
    But yours it seems have yet that art to learn.'
Then rose there to the view—but not beneath
    The chin disclosed—near where he stood—the shade
    Of one who seem'd to rest upon his knees. [4]

---

[3] ' The ancestors of Dante, and Dante himself, were Guelfs. He did
not become a Ghibelline till after his banishment.' Longfellow.
[4] Cavalcante Cavalcanti.

Round me he gazed a while, as tho' he were   55

    Intent to know if any came with me :

    But, when his surmise was all spent, with tears

He thus exclaim'd ; ' If thro' this prison-house

    Thou goest by loftiness of mind, O say—

    My son—where is he ? and wherefore not with thee ?' 60

To whom I answer'd ; ' Of myself I come not,

    But led by him who tarries there—one whom

    Perhaps thy Guido[5] held in light esteem.'

His language and his mode of punishment

    Already had reveal'd to me his name ;   65

    Whence my response was thus complete.   Thereon

Suddenly to his feet he sprang, and cried ;

    ' How said'st thou " *held* in light esteem ? " Lives he

    Not then ?   Falls not Heaven's blessed light upon

His eyes ? '   When he was conscious of some slight   70

    Delay that intervened before I made

    Response, he fell back, and was seen no more.

But he of stronger mind, at whose request

    I linger'd, neither changed his countenance,

    Nor moved his neck, nor from his state inclined.   75

---

[5] Guido Cavalcanti was more addicted to philosophy than to poetry. And, as a Guelf, he would naturally be hostile to the teaching of Virgil, the poet of the Empire.

'And if,' said he, his former speech renewing,

   'They have but ill acquired that art of thine,

   More than this fiery couch that thought torments me.

But ere the face of her who ruleth here [6]

   Hath been refill'd with light the fiftieth time,   80

   Thou shalt behold what progress they have made.

And—so may'st thou to the sweet world return—

   Say for what cause that state [7] in all its laws

   Pursues my people with such rancorous hate ?'

Whence I replied ; 'The slaughter, and the great   85

   Havoc, that dyed with crimson Arbia's waters, [8]

   Are not forgotten in our temples yet.' [9]

Then heaved he a deep sigh, and shook his head,

   And ' I was not alone in that,' he said ;

   ' Nor without cause moved I with the others then :   90

But there [10] I was alone, where 'twas by all

   Consented to raze Florence to the ground :

   'Twas I defended her before them all.'

---

[6] 'The moon, called in the heavens Diana, on earth Luna, and in the infernal regions Proserpina.' Longfellow.

[7] Florence.

[8] The battle of Monte Aperto, near the river Arbia, in which the Guelfs were routed by the Ghibellines, who were commanded by Farinata.

[9] Prayers for deliverance from the Uberti were offered up in the Churches of Florence. Public deliberations were held in the Churches. Either of these facts may have been referred to in this line.

Again I spake ; ' So may thy people find

    Repose in other days—resolve for me   95

    This doubt, which wraps me in a wildering maze :

It seems, if I hear rightly, that you see

    Beforehand that which time brings on with it,

    While of things present you are unaware ? '

' We see, as those who have defective sight,'   100

    He answer'd, ' things which are from us remote :

    So much of light the sovran Lord vouchsafes.

When they are near, or present, vanish'd quite

    Is that foreknowledge ; and, unless inform'd,

    We have no knowledge of your actual state.   105

Whence easily thou may'st infer that all

    Our power of knowing will expire, when once

    The portal of futurity is closed.'

Then for my negligence [10] contrition feeling

    I said ; ' Now speak to him who there lies fallen,   110

    And say his son is yet among the living :

And if before I linger'd in replying,

    Tell him that I was mentally revolving

    This doubt, which thy solution has resolved.'

---

[10] At the diet of the Ghibellines assembled, after the battle of Monte Aperto, by Guido Novello at Empoli.

[11] In not answering Cavalcante's question contained in v. 69.

And now to me I heard the Master calling ;   115
   Whence I besought the spirit with more haste
   To tell me who were prison'd in the vaults.
And he replied ; 'More than a thousand here
   Are placed: here lies the second Frederick ;[12] there
   The Cardinal :[13] I speak not of the rest.'   120
This said, he vanish'd : I thereon towards
   The Bard my steps retraced, pondering the while
   That mystic speech[14] which seem'd to threaten ill.
Onward he moved, and, as we paced along,
   This question put to me ; 'Wherefore art thou   125
   So lost in thought ?'   I his request fulfill'd.
'Let thy mind treasure up that which the spirit
   Reveal'd against thyself,' enjoin'd the sage,
   And here 'Attend' he said, with hand uplifted.
'When thou shalt rest beneath the radiant vision   130
   Of her, whose bright eye seëth all things, thou
   Wilt hear from her all thy life's pilgrimage.'

---

[12] Frederick II., grandson of Barbarossa, Emperor of Germany, and King of Naples and Sicily.

[13] Cardinal Ottaviano Ubaldini, called 'the Cardinal' on account of his great influence.   All these persons, viz., Farinata, Cavalcante, Frederick II., and Cardinal Ubaldini, held Epicurean opinions.

[14] Farinata's prediction in v. 79-81.

He therewith turning to the left hand, we left

    The wall ; then 'mid the tombs in haste we wended

    Along a path which strikes upon a valley,   135

Whose noxious fumes ev'n to that height ascended.

BIBLIOBAZAAR

The essential book market!

Did you know that you can get any of our titles in our trademark **EasyRead**™ print format? **EasyRead**™ provides readers with a larger than average typeface, for a reading experience that's easier on the eyes.

Did you know that we have an ever-growing collection of books in many languages?

Order online:
www.bibliobazaar.com

Or to exclusively browse our **EasyRead**™ collection:
www.bibliogrande.com

At BiblioBazaar, we aim to make knowledge more accessible by making thousands of titles available to you – quickly and affordably.

Contact us:
BiblioBazaar
PO Box 21206
Charleston, SC 29413

CPSIA information can be obtained at www.ICGtesting.com
Printed in the USA
BVOW061340090812

297496BV00003B/29/P

9 780554 539362